With the Leader's Guide

More Than Skin Deep

Marcia Dorris & Kim Dishroon

Unless otherwise noted, Scripture quotations are
from the Holy Bible, New Living Translation
copyright 1996 by Tyndale Charitable Trust.
Scripture quotations identified NIV are from the New International
Version, copyright 1973, 1978, 1984 by International Bible Society.
Scripture quotations identified by Message are from the MESSAGE
Bible copyright 2004 by the Zondervan Corporation.
Scripture quotations identified by Word on the Street
are from The Word on the Street Version, copyright
2003, 2004 formerly the Street Bible by Rob Lacey.
Other references include The New Strong's Expanded
Exhaustive Concordance of the Bible, this will be indicated
by the Greek or Hebrew words enclosed in <brackets>.
 Zondervan's Bible Dictionary is also quoted and referenced.

ISBN
978-1-964488-11-0 (Paperback)
978-1-964488-12-7 (eBook)

TABLE OF CONTENTS

ACKNOWLEDGEMENTS

Special thank you to all the youth workers who helped make our inaugural weekend retreat such a success.

Thank you to Xavier Jasso and Muse Mind Studios for his creative eye in shooting the front and back cover photos.

Jessica Demarco of TRU2U salon you are amazing! Thank you for donating your time and talents.

Elizabeth Goggans Newbould without your help with childcare we couldn't have accomplished this project. We appreciate your encouragement every step of the way.

Brandi Dixon your literary knowledge and wisdom have been such a huge help to us in the finalizing of this study.

Cody Widdows without your help we wouldn't have a website. You are a rockstar!!

Thanks Kelsey Widdows for your willingness to be our cover model. Your beauty is truly more than skin deep.

20/20 Literary Group thank you for taking this project on and bringing our dream to life.

ATTENTION LEADERS

This study can be done as a weekend getaway or a weekly bible study. Either way it is designed to be worked on together as a group with as much group interaction as possible.

The skits can be done by the leaders or whomever you have to do them. They are silly but should bring the scripture to life in new and memorable ways for the young ladies. *Desire and Deception* is a short movie script and would be great if you are able to video it prior to doing the Section on Cleansing.

Taking advantage of the games, skits and activities will help reinforce the lessons in each section.

Instructions for all games, skits, and activities can be found in the appendix.

 Demos will be denoted with Daisy.

 Games and Activities will be denoted with an art palette.

 Skits will be denoted with a clapperboard.

See our website for additional resources
www.skindeepbiblestudy.com.

BEAUTY BASICS

 Finger painting activity

What do you know about the fountain of youth? Who was the explorer who spent much of his life and money in search of it? Where was the fountain of youth supposedly located?

Ponce de Leon searched for years for the miraculous waters. Legend had it that anyone who bathed or drank from the fountain of youth would never grow old. Throughout centuries man has been searching for the fountain of youth. He has been diligently seeking ways to stay youthful and attractive.

Today we are still searching for a beauty treatment that will keep us young and gorgeous forever. There are skin care products and enhancement services everywhere you look. The checkout counters in many stores are lined with magazines of beauty tips to get you noticed. TikTok is full of products and how-to's, all with the claim that they will enhance your best beauty features.

The traditional beauty shops where your grandmother went to get her "hair done" are now called salons, or day spas, which offer treatments for virtually every part of your body. For the right price you can get teeth whitening, lip plumping, brow waxing, and body piercing. There are injections to put things in that are missing, liposuction to take things out that you don't want, body wraps to melt parts away and enhancement surgeries to add to other parts.

When you hear the word beautiful, who do you think of?

What makes them beautiful?

What is your definition of beauty?

As a small child, one looks at her mother as the most beautiful person in the world. As she gets a little older, she sees the fairy tale princesses with their tiaras as her definition of beauty. Upon entering the teenage years, she looks to the Hollywood actresses and social media for her image. When she matures into a married, young lady and is carrying her firstborn child, her husband sees her as beauty personified, even though she feels like a beached whale. The moment she sees her newborn baby, she has redefined beauty. At the first sign of gray hair and wrinkles, the search begins to find an anti-aging regimen that will make her look attractive once again.

What is beauty and where can we find it? If we look on the Internet, we can find 6 million websites that can help find the beauty treatment that will supposedly transform you into the supermodel you always hoped to be.

Webster's Dictionary defines beauty as having _____

_____ and _____ _____ _____.

The world teaches that if you look good on the outside, then you will feel good on the inside. There are plenty of examples to dispel this notion. You can see it by the terrible way some celebrities treat people. Think about a particular supermodel and the awful manner she treated young ladies on social media. She was looked upon as the picture of beauty, but her treatment of others showed she wasn't as happy as one might think. Those who sincerely feel good on the inside generally build others up. Many times, in reality these beautiful celebrities who many young people look up to and admire are unhappy, unfulfilled and not attractive on the inside.

On a youth mission trip while working with teenagers from around the country there was a young lady who upon first meeting everyone admired her outer beauty. She was absolutely gorgeous on the outside but the more we were around her and saw the mean, rude way she interacted with others she became less and less attractive. By the end of the week no one thought she was the least bit pretty. There was another young lady who upon first glance wasn't the prettiest girl in the room but because she had such a great attitude and was so helpful and kind, she became more and more attractive as the week progressed.

We don't want to get our definition of beauty from Hollywood or Wikipedia.

We want to get our definition of beauty from the one who created beauty.

The first beauty pageant recorded is found in the pages of the Old Testament. The year was 479 BC, and the setting was the Persian empire. Queen Vashti had just been dethroned because of disobedience and King Xerxes had been advised to have a beauty pageant to find her successor.

The entire Persian empire was full of nervous energy and anticipation as each young maiden had hopes of becoming the next "Miss Persia." After the finalists had been selected, they were sent to the Susa beauty spa for a complete year of beauty treatments. To add to the excitement, they found out that the judge of the pageant was none other than King Xerxes himself, and not only would the winner wear the tiara, but would also be married to the most powerful man in the Persian empire.

The maidens of Persia spent a year of intense treatments, preparing to meet the king face-to-face.

> **Jesus is our king and we as Christians are his bride. We need to take time out of our busy schedules for some intense beauty treatments to prepare us to meet him face-to-face.**

During this study, we will begin a makeover by applying various beauty products and principles that can transform us from the inside out.

We will learn steps not only to begin a physical beauty routine but more importantly ways to enhance our relationship with Jesus and others.

CLEANSING

For our extreme makeover, we need to start out with a clean slate. To do this, we must remove any existing makeup and residue. We will be using a cleansing agent which will clear away the surface oils and dirt. This is a *gentle* cleanser that will only remove the superficial impurities and will leave your face feeling soft and refreshed.

 ### Cleansing demo

Our society has a desire to look attractive. This is proven by all the cleaning services and products available to us. We have car washes, maid services, laundromats, carpet cleaners, hand soaps, body scrubs, detergents, dishwashers, dog groomers, street sweepers, hot tubs, and the list goes on.

What could be motivating us to have our bodies and possessions in a state of cleanliness? Is it just the pride of our neighbor seeing our things sparkle and shine, or is there a deeper need?

 ### Dirty cup demo

Should we only be concerned about how we look on the outside? Why or why not?

What was more important? For the cup to look pretty on the outside or to be clean on the inside?

When you choose your friends, are you more concerned about how they dress and what they look like or do you look deeper?

When God looks at you, He sees your heart and how you look on the inside.

When you think about who you might one day marry, what is more important to you; their physical appearance or what their inner qualities are? Write down qualities you might be looking for:

How often do we ask our friends questions like: How do I look? Do I have mascara under my eyes? Does this dress make me look fat? Is my hair sticking up in the back? Does this shirt go with these pants? Do my shoes match my outfit?

We are constantly asking for feedback about our appearance, but how often do we ask questions about our character?

How did I treat her? Did I hurt his feelings? Have we ignored her? What did my expressions really tell her?

Do you ever evaluate how you act towards other people, or do you only focus on your outer appearance?

Matthew 23:25b NLT

> *Jesus said to the religious leaders and Pharisees, "You are so careful to clean the outside of the cup and the dish, but inside you are filthy– full of greed and self-indulgence!"*

When the world looks at you, how clean do you appear?

As God examines your heart, what does He find?

Desire and Deception Part 1

Earlier, when we were painting our portraits and first dipped our fingers in the paint, we really took notice of the gooey, slimy paint that oozed up between our fingers and messed up our perfectly manicured nails. But as we got more involved in our artwork, we became less aware of the mess and more focused on the masterpiece we were creating.

When we first get involved in sinful behavior, our conscience really bothers us. However, after ignoring the convictions of the Holy Spirit, it becomes such a part of us that we hardly take notice of it. Committing one sin usually leads us to other sin such as lying and deception in order to cover up the first sin we committed.

🎬 Desire and Deception Part 2

Isaiah 59:2–3 (NIV)

> *"Your iniquities have separated you from your God;*
> *your sins have hidden his face from you, so that he*
> *will not hear. For your hands are stained with blood,*
> *your fingers with guilt. Your lips have spoken lies,*
> *and your tongue mutters wicked things."*

How does it make you feel to know God sees everything you do and knows every thought you have, even those you wouldn't dare speak out loud to anyone?

God created each of us. Whether we recognize it or not, we do have a need to be in a right relationship with the Lord. After Adam and Eve were first created, God would come into the garden and fellowship with them. He told them that they could eat from any tree in the garden: the apples, pears, peaches, mangoes, oranges, papaya, cherries, and so many other choices. There was only one exception…

🎬 Adam and Eve Skit Part 1

As you've seen through this humorous interpretation of scripture, there are consequences to our sinful behavior. Adam and Eve were ashamed of their actions, which brought knowledge of their uncleanliness before God. Because of the wrong choice they made, their fellowship with the Lord was broken.

Briefly describe a time when you did something that was wrong and you damaged a relationship. (This could be with parents, siblings, friends, etc.)

How did it make you feel?

What did you do to resolve the situation?

If you have not resolved it, describe how you feel about the situation now.

🎬 Adam and Eve Skit Part 2

The first step to mending a broken relationship is to "come clean" about our actions. Do we take full responsibility for our actions or do we, like our unfashionable friends, acknowledge our sinful behavior, but blame someone else for it? *"Lord, I know it's wrong to hate people, but it's really not my fault because she didn't invite me to her party,"* or *"She was flirting with my boyfriend,"* or *"She's always talking about me and giving me dirty looks."* It doesn't matter what the other person did, the Lord will look at your actions, and how you portray his love to others.

> **Psalm 32:5 NLT**
>
> **Finally, I confessed all my sins to you and stopped trying to hide them. I said to myself, "I will confess my rebellion to the Lord," and you forgave me! All my guilt is gone.**

Have you ever tried to "hide" your sins?

How does it make you feel when you try to hide things from others?

God is our Father, and we need to stay open and honest with Him. When we accept Jesus as our Lord and Savior, God adopts us as daughters, and He wants us all to be "daddy's girl." As a little girl, we always wanted to make our daddies proud. As children of God, we should always want to please Him because of our love for Him.

> **2 Corinthians 6:18 through 7:1**
>
> *And I will be your_____, and you will be my_____, and_____, says the Lord Almighty. Because we have these _____, dear friends, let us _____ ourselves from everything that can_____ our body or spirit. And let us work toward_____*
>
> *because we fear God.*

In the above verse, the Strong's word for fear is the Greek word "Phobos" (fob-os) *which means:*

"_____ _____ _____ ____

_____ _____."

How do we become clean? Look at the following verses, and let's find out.

1 John 1:9

> *But if we confess our sins to Him, He is faithful and just to forgive us, and to cleanse us from every wrong.*

What does 1 John 1:9 say we must do in order to be cleansed?

Greek word for "cleanse" <2511> katharizo (kath-ar-id-zo) means to "make clean, be clean, purge, purify– to cleanse from the defilement of sin and guilt."

Titus 2:14

> *He gave his life to free us from every kind of sin, to cleanse us, and to make us His very own people, totally committed to doing what is right.*

According to Titus, give the three reasons that Jesus gave His life for us.

2 Timothy 2:21

> *If you keep yourself pure, you will be a special utensil for honorable use. Your life will be clean, and you will be ready for the master to use you for every good work.*

What did God promise in this verse if you keep yourself pure?

The Greek word for "pure" <1571> **ekkathairo** (ek-kat<u>h</u>-<u>ak</u>-ee-ro)

means "_____ _____ _____,

_____ _____,_____

_____."

Hebrews 10:22

> *Let us go right into the presence of God, with true*
> *hearts, fully trusting Him. For our evil conscience has*
> *been sprinkled with Christ's blood to make us clean,*
> *and our bodies have been washed with pure water.*

How should we go into the presence of God?

What is it that makes us clean before God?

Notice the verse says, "let us **go** right into the presence of God." It doesn't say knock before entering, it doesn't tell us to go through the Virgin Mary or confess our sins to a priest. We are to go right into His presence with our hearts fully trusting Him. King David was a man after God's own heart; in fact, David had so much trust in the Lord that he was able to say to the Lord:

Psalm 17:3 (The Message)

> *Go ahead, examine me from inside out, surprise me*
> *in the middle of the night- you'll find I'm just what*
> *I say I am.*

Could you, as the Psalmist did, take this personal challenge?

We want to enter into the presence of God. We hope you can already feel His spirit with us. We have washed our faces now, let us take a few minutes to cleanse our hearts.

Spend some time with the Lord in prayer. Ask Him what specific sins you need to confess to Him. Write down your prayer to God at the end of this section. Also, write down what you believe the Lord may be saying to you. This is your personal book for you to keep, and this prayer is only between you and the Lord.

(Prayer time to examine ourselves. Ask God to reveal what you may need to be cleansed from.)

 Hand Out Markers for Sins Demo

> *Psalm 24:4–5*
>
> > **He who has clean hands and a pure heart, who does not lift up his soul to an idol, or swear by what is false. He will receive blessings from the Lord and vindication from God his Savior.**

Song suggestion "Come to the Altar" or "Give us Clean Hands"

 Finish Sins Demo

Prayer, Notes and Reflection

_____

_____

_____

_____

_____

_____

_____

_____

_____

_____

_____

_____

_____

_____

_____

_____

DEEP CLEANSING

Daily washing is an important step to fresh looking skin, but the surface of our face is not the only place that dirt and oil accumulate. Our skin is porous, which means we have tiny openings in which impurities can hide. The cells that make up skin constantly develop, grow, and die. These dead skin cells and hidden gunk, deep within our pores, cause the skin to look dull, tired, and blotchy. Periodically, we need to use a facial scrub. Many of these are clay-based. The clay pulls the deep dirt and oil out from the pores and absorbs it in tiny sand like particles. This helps exfoliate the dead surface cells to re-texture and smooth the skin.

 Face Mask Demo

This mask will leave the face totally clean and radiant. In our spiritual life, it's important for us to be totally clean and honest before God. Remember, He made us, He knows our every thought in our innermost being. We have just applied a mask to our face literally, but how many different masks do you wear on a regular basis?

Name some situations that would make someone act like someone or something that they are not.

Do you act like the same person when you're with your friends at church as you do with your school friends, or the friends that think Christians are "uncool?" Do you present yourself in the same fashion in the mall as you would in a worship service? Does your vocabulary at a Friday night football game imitate your vocabulary in your Christian group? Have you been wearing your mask so long that you have forgotten what the real you looks like? Or have you gotten so comfortable behind your mask that you can't imagine facing the world without it? Maybe you have built such a reputation around your mask that you're afraid of losing your friends if you take it off. If so, they really aren't your friends in the first place.

When have you tried to be someone you were not?

What were your reasons?

How differently did you treat others?

Did you feel good about yourself?

 Mask Activity- write on the inside of them some reasons that would make you wear a mask.

1 John 5:19

Dear children, keep away from anything that might take God's place in your hearts.

What possessions or hobbies would you cry about if you had to give them up?

What types of things or activities can people set up as idols in their lives?

What determines if something is an idol in a person's life?

What has the potential to become an idol in your life, and how can you prevent that from happening?

Who are you really trying to impress? Who is the most important person in your life? Have you made your friends your idol and put Jesus in the background in case of emergencies? Who are all of these masks for? This type of charade is deceptive as well as self-destructive. This, along with other types of "concealers" needs to be scraped away, or exfoliated from your life.

> **Ezekiel 36:25**
>
> **I will sprinkle clean water on you, and you will be clean; I will cleanse you from all your impurities and from all your idols.**

What does the scripture say that Jesus wants to do for us?

How have you allowed Him to do this for you?

What is it that you're hanging onto and not willing to let him take from you?

 Penny Story

There was a lady in her kitchen cooking dinner one afternoon. Her six-year-old son was playing quietly in the living room. All of a sudden, she heard him crying and screaming so she ran into the living room where he was. She found him sitting on the couch with his hand down a flower vase. She tried to pull it off his hand and realized the reason he was crying was that his hand was stuck in the vase. The mother tried to calm him down and told him she would rub some lotion on his arm and the vase would probably slip right off. This didn't work and the boy became even more hysterical, he began waving his arm around, trying to shake the vase off. His mother stopped him and began explaining that they needed to be very careful getting his hand out because this was a priceless vase her great grandfather had made. He was a famous potter in Germany years ago and had made this, one of a kind, vase for his wife and it had been passed down through generations to her.

All of a sudden, the little boy jerked his arm and the vase hit the coffee table and shattered into a million pieces. His mother, with tears in her eyes, looked down and saw her son with his fist gripped tight. She unclenched his hand and saw he was holding a penny. She asked her son why he had not unclenched his hand so it could slide out of

19

the vase. He said he didn't want to lose what he was holding.

Are you giving up something priceless because you are holding on to something worthless?

Adapted from the story by Helmut Tielicke, German Theologian

 ## Begin Idol Activity

Write down on one piece of paper one or more things that God would consider an idol in your life. This is anything that will cause your thoughts or actions to draw you away from the Lord. Please pray about what the Lord is asking you to give to Him. Do not take this lightly; this is serious business between you and the Lord.

(go somewhere quiet to think and pray)

Prayer notes
_____
_____
_____
_____
_____
_____

Idols will not automatically vanish from your life. You have to actively guard against these things creeping back in. Now on another piece of paper, write down active ways to prevent these things from having control over you; such as not hanging out with friends who use foul language and talk about things that cause you to have unclean thoughts. Stop acting in certain ways so you can be included in "the group." Don't spend time alone with a boyfriend that pulls you away from positive influences and puts sexual pressure on you. Don't be best friends with anyone who desires you to do things to destroy your mind and body (like smoking, drinking, sex, cutting yourself, drugs, wild parties, profanity, and malicious talk).

 ### Finish Idol Activity

As we watched the fire consume our idols, we could see the smoke rising. If you were honest and sincere with the Lord about what you wanted to be rid of, then your "burnt offering" will be acceptable to Him. You can look at this as a form of prayer. As the smoke goes toward heaven, so did your confession to Him.

When we admit our sins to God, He knows if it is just a confession or a true repentance. Confession is the first step to repentance, but we can confess without truly repenting. Confession is to admit to God and agree with Him that a specific action or lifestyle is wrong according to His word. We can confess and agree with Him about a specific sin, and still not change our actions. How often do you find yourself confessing the same sins day after day?

In the book of Exodus, God set into motion a plan to give the Israelites freedom from the Egyptians. Through a servant named Moses, God commanded Pharaoh to let His people go. Pharaoh and the Egyptians refused and God made their lives even more unbearable. God began to send plagues upon the people of Egypt. There were 10 different plagues that were released upon the land. After the seventh plague, the following conversation took place between Moses and Pharaoh:

Confession vs Repentance

Exodus 9:27

> *Then, Pharaoh urgently sent for Moses and Aaron. "I finally admit my fault," he confessed. "The Lord is right, and my people and I are wrong."*

What did Pharaoh say?

Did he confess his sins?

Does it seem that Pharaoh had a change of heart?

Exodus 9:28–29

Please beg the Lord to end this terrifying, thunder and hail; I will let you go at once.

Briefly describe a time when you confessed your sin before God and begged Him to release you from the consequences and promise to do better.

Exodus 9:34 (The Message)

But once Pharaoh saw that the rain and hail and thunder had stopped, he kept right on sinning, stubborn as ever, both he and his servants. Pharaoh's heart turned rock hard. He refused to release the Israelites, as God had ordered through Moses.

They confessed and asked for mercy, but were they truly repentant?

When pharaoh got what he wanted, he went right back to his old ways. In your situation when you begged for mercy and made promises to God to change, which promises did you keep?

MORE THAN SKIN DEEP

Which promises did you break?

What is the difference between confession and repentance?

Now that we have a clear understanding of what confession is, let's take a look at repentance.

> **Zondervan Bible dictionary,
> defines repentance as:**
>
> "_____
>
> _____ _____
>
> _____ _____ _____
>
> _____ _____"

When we truly repent of our sins, then we will turn from evil ways to God's ways.

> **Acts 3:19**
>
> *Now turn from your sins and turn to God, so you can be cleansed of your sins.*

Strong's word for "<u>turn</u>" is the Greek word mitanoeo (met-an-o-eh-o) <3340> it is the same word for <u>repent</u> which means:

To change one's _____ or _____. A

_____for the _____.

There are three steps involved:

1) gaining new_____.

2) Regret for your _____and a displeasure with _____.

3) A change of_____.

Strong's word for cleansed is the Greek word exaleipho <1813> (ex-Al-I-fo) this word means:

To_____ and_____ to_____ or

_____ _____, to _____ _____,

_____ _____, completely_____.

As you can see, to have true repentance you have to not only admit your sin, but you should also be brokenhearted over displeasing your heavenly Father. The result of this would be a desire to walk with Him and to be set free from the sin that entangles you.

Now, let's tune in and find out what is going on in the lives of David and Bathsheba.

🎬 Desire and Deception Part 3

Nathan painted David a vivid picture of his actions. This enabled God's words to penetrate David by reflecting his heart, like a mirror, and exposing his sinful deeds. After David's repentance, he wrote Psalm 32. Let's take a look at it and see what lessons he learned.

Psalm 32:3–5

> *When I refused to confess my sin, my body wasted away, and I groaned all day long. Day and night Your hand of discipline was heavy on me. My strength evaporated like water in the summer heat. Finally, I confessed all my sins to You and stopped trying to hide my guilt. I said to myself, "I will confess my rebellion to the Lord." And You forgave me! All my guilt is gone.*

What effect can confessing have on you?

Why did David say that the Lord's hand of discipline was heavy on him?

Can you relate to how David was feeling? Explain why or why not.

Think back to the story of the plagues and Pharaoh. What was the end result of ***Pharaoh's*** *confession?*

What was the end result for ***David's*** *confession?*

What was the difference?

Pharaoh confessed only to save himself from the wrath of the Lord, he did not intend to change his lifestyle. David confessed out of a conviction of sin and remorse for dishonoring the Lord. He was brokenhearted over his wrongdoing and the many lives it affected.

Psalm 51:17

The _____ you

want is a broken _____ .

A _____ and

_____ _____

oh, God, you _____ _____

_____ .

Because of David's honest confession, in total repentance, he had a renewed sense of joy. He had been set free from the guilt and bondage of his sinful behavior.

Scrub away my guilt, soak me in your laundry, and I'll come out clean, scrub me, and I'll have a "Snow White" life. Think about Snow White's life. Yes, she did have some difficulties and trials, and, like Eve, she suffered from eating the wrong fruit. However, in the end much the same as Esther, she did end up with her prince. We, too, will spend eternity with our prince of peace if we confess Him as our Lord and repent of our sins. He is planning the biggest party of all time and anyone who is cool will be there. In fact, if you're not there, you will be really, really hot.

Pray this as a closing prayer for this session:

Psalm 51 (The Message)

Generous in love, God, give us grace and mercy—wipe out my bad record. Scrub away my guilt; soak out my sins in your laundry. I know how bad I've been; my sins are staring me down. You're the one I violated, and you've seen it all, seeing the full extent of my evil. You have all the facts before you; whatever you decide about me is fair. I've been out of step with you for a long time; in the wrong, since before I was born. What you're after is truth from the inside out. Enter me, then conceive a new, true life.

While we are still in a spirit of prayer, fill in the blanks below.

My sins of_____have

been wiped away on_____ (date)

_____

(signature)

Psalm 32:1–2

Oh, what joy for those whose rebellion is forgiven, whose sin is out of sight! Yes, what joy for those whose record the Lord has cleared of sin, whose lives are lived in complete honesty.

Psalm 32:11 from the message tells us to:

Celebrate God, sing together- everyone! All you honest hearts raise the roof!

Song Suggestion "Let it Rise."

If you have free time after this section, use it to decorate your masks.

FRESHENER

(Part One)

The next phase in our beauty regimen is to apply freshener. This step will promote the elasticity and firmness of your skin, while also energizing the skin cells and bringing about a radiant, renewed look.

Freshener Demo on one girl furnish supplies for others

Along with rejuvenating and firming your skin, the freshener will also remove any residue left over from wearing your mask. Looking at one another, it appears that our masks are gone. But sometimes you can feel the remaining particles still on your face. If you don't completely remove them from your face, then before you know it....

🎬 Parade of Fakes Skit Part 1

If you were trying to find your identity from any other source than in your Creator, then you are setting yourself up for some major disappointments and trouble in life.

🎬 Parade of Fakes Skit Part 2

As little girls, it was fun to play dress up and pretend. We were doctors, teachers, and famous actresses. Now that we are growing up, we need to start becoming the person we were intended to be. All of us at some time or another have wished we were different. If we have straight hair, we want curly hair. If we are short, we wish we were tall. If we have brown hair, we want blonde. We want to be singers, cheerleaders, part of the "in" crowd; none of us are ever truly satisfied with who we are inside or out. By spending time and energy trying to change who we really are, we are sending God a message that He must have messed up when He made us. We are not only insulting God; we are also robbing ourselves of becoming the most beautiful princesses that God designed each of us to be. We know this truth is difficult to grasp at this point in your life, but if you can learn to focus on your strong points, then you can be content with what the Lord has given you. You can accept yourself as the priceless treasure that you were created to be.

(Optional- Hand out mirrors to each girl to keep)

Take a minute and look at yourself in the mirror and say some positive phrases about your inner beauty. Examples: I am a priceless treasure; I am loved; I am marvelously made.

Psalm 139:13–18

Oh, yes, You shaped me first inside, then out; You formed me in my mother's womb. I thank you, high God— you're breathtaking! Body and soul, I am marvelously made! I worship in adoration— what a creation!

Name some of your strong points.

List some ways to take advantage of your strong points.

List some ways the Lord can use your strengths.

Name some things you would consider your weaknesses.

Give some examples of how God can use your weaknesses.

 Affirmation Game

Another benefit of using a freshener is the enhancement of the skin's firmness and elasticity. Women spend millions of dollars each year on beauty products that promise them younger looking skin. Browse the cosmetic aisles of any store or notice the targeted ads on YouTube, and you will see how society is bombarding us with the so-called need to have that "cover girl" look. Can you name some products and services that promote this obsession? (Chemical peels, anti-aging creams, injections and surgical facelifts). In a sense, we could learn a valuable lesson from these beauty crazed fanatics. We should have the same type of desperation in seeking a firm foundation in our faith.

 Money Game

Give some words and phrases to describe your hunt for the hidden treasure. Did you let anything get in your way?

Did you allow unbelieving bystanders to distract you in your search? Just how desperate were you to find the money?

Those who found the money please read the verses on the back of the money to the group.

We need to have the same kind of hunger for finding God as we did while we were searching for the money. Do we chase after the Lord with the same kind of excitement?

Rate the next two questions on a scale of 1-10.

How bad did you want to win the prize?

*How eager are you to really **know** the Lord?*

Let's spend a few minutes in prayer asking the Lord how He would have scored us on this last question.

Prayer Reflection and Notes

FRESHENER

(Part Two)

 Race with Weights

Isaiah 40: 29–31

He gives_____ to the_____ and increases the_____ of the_____. Even_____ grow_____ and_____ and young men_____ and_____. But those who_____ in the Lord will_____ their_____. They will_____ on wings like_____, they will run and not grow_____ they will walk and not be_____.

Think about the race; why was it harder for team B than for team A? Wouldn't it have been easier for you if you had not put on the weights? Why did you wear them if you knew they would slow you down? Do you ever take bad advice from others?

Just like the weights in our race, many times our disappointments in life can weigh us down. Such as being rejected by friends, being made fun of, a lack of acceptance from others, difficult home life, always seeming to come in last place, physical limitations, and broken relationships. These are just a few of the things that can have a negative effect on our spiritual, emotional, and physical well-being. How do we combat these external attacks on our internal beings? Too many times when others hurt us our fleshly reaction is quick and severe retaliation.

Write down a time when you were hurt or disappointed by someone.

What was your immediate reaction to the situation?

Proverbs 15:26 (The Message Bible) God can't stand evil scheming, but he puts words of grace and beauty on display.

After you have had time to think about the situation and cool off, how did you respond?

Was it the same or different from your initial reaction?

1 Peter 2:1–3 (Word on the Street translation)

> *Click delete on the software that makes you mean-minded, forked– tongue, two-faced, green eyed, and foul mouth. They are like babies, crying out, desperate for spiritual milk– it's the only way to grow in your liberation, now that you've sampled God's appetizer.*

> *Ephesians 5:26–27 (The Message paraphrase) Christ's love makes us whole. His (Jesus) words evoke beauty. Everything He does and says is designed to bring out our best.*

Developing a confidence in ourselves and being happy with who we are in Christ will be a protective shield against the evil words and actions of others. As the saying goes: *I am rubber, you are glue, anything you call me, bounces off me and sticks on you.*

The most powerful weapon to fight worldly attacks is living inside each Christian. It is the Holy Spirit. God's Spirit will constantly direct our actions, *if* we will ask and allow Him to. Beginning each day with prayer by asking Him to clothe us with His armor will help us get ready for the day. Tape a card with the armor of God scripture to your mirror to read while getting ready in the mornings. Develop some friendships with other Christians who will be faithful to uplift you and will lovingly call attention to any steps you take off the right path. In return, you need to strive to be a faithful friend to others as well.

Think about your friendships right now, your close friends. How many true friends do you have that are committed Christians and would be willing to call you out if need be?

Proverbs 12:26

The godly give good advice to their friends; the wicked lead them astray.

What type of people do you seek out to be your friends and confidants?

Proverbs 27:9 (The Message)

Just as lotions and fragrance give sensual delight, a sweet friendship refreshes the soul.

Are you looking for someone to just have fun with or someone who will help direct you in your walk with the Lord?

As we mature and grow into becoming the princess He created us to be, we will learn to be thankful for the trials we have gone through. We should be able to look deeper into conflicts that arise and learn how to resolve the differences between us while still maintaining our friendships. The Bible tells us that we are allowed to go through difficult times in order to strengthen our relationship with Him.

The Teacup

There was once a couple who liked to shop at antique stores and collect cups. For their 50th wedding anniversary they took a trip to England. They had heard of a great antique shop that specialized in unique tea cups. On every anniversary for 24 years, the husband bought his wife a beautiful antique teacup. This year's had to be extra special because it was their golden wedding anniversary.

After arriving in London and finding an antique shop they had heard so much about, they spotted the perfect tea cup, displayed in grandeur behind the glass of a large, cherry, curio cabinet. The couple asked, "May we see this one? We've never seen a cup, quite so beautiful."

As a lady handed it to them, suddenly the tea cup began to speak, "I haven't always been beautiful," it said. "In fact, I haven't always been a teacup. There was a time when I was just a lump of red clay. My master took me in, rolled me, pounded, and patted me over and over. I yelled for him to stop, but he just smiled, and gently said, 'not yet.'"

"Then wham! I was placed on a spinning wheel and was spun around and around. 'Stop it! I'm getting dizzy! I'm going to be sick!' But the master only nodded and quietly said, 'Not yet.'"

"He spun, poked, and prodded at me, then, bam! He put me in the oven, and I had never felt such heat. I yelled, and pounded on the door for him to let me out. He just shook his head, and quietly said, 'Not yet.'"

"When I thought I couldn't bear another minute, the door opened. He carefully took me out and put me on the shelf to cool. Oh, it felt so good. But, after a while, he picked me up and started brushing and painting all over me. The paint fumes smelled terrible. I thought I would gag. Then, suddenly, back in the oven, I went. This time it was even hotter. I just knew I was going to suffocate! I begged and pleaded to get out of there, but once again, he shook his head gently, and said softly, ' "Not yet.'"

"I was convinced I would never survive this. I was ready to give up; I just could not take any more. At that very moment, the door opened. My master carefully lifted me out and placed me back on the shelf to cool for a while. I sat enjoying the rest, but wondering what was going to happen to me next. Then, with a smile on his face, my master handed me a mirror, and said, 'Look at yourself.'"

"That's not me!" I exclaimed. "That's beautiful! I am beautiful!" Quietly he spoke, "I want you to remember, when you were being rolled and pounded, if I had left you alone, you would've dried up, when you were dizzy, spinning, around and around if I had stopped, you would've crumpled, I know it hurt when it was hot in the oven, but if I hadn't put you through the fire, you would have cracked. I know the paint fumes were bad, but if I hadn't done that, you would not have any color in your life. Now you are a finished product. Now you are what I had planned for you, now you are beautiful."

Author unknown.

1 Peter 1:6–7

> *So be truly glad! There is wonderful joy ahead, even though it is necessary for you to endure many trials for a while. These trials are only to test your faith, to show that it is strong and pure. It is being tested as fire tests and purifies gold. Your faith is far more precious to God than gold. So if your faith remains strong after being tested by fiery trials, it will bring you much praise and glory and honor on the day when Jesus Christ is revealed to the whole world.*

The source of this joy is the Holy Spirit. Just like when we're thirsty, we will fill up a glass of water and drink it. We need to fill ourselves up with the Holy Spirit when our souls are dry and weary. This is done through prayer and spiritual disciplines. Now let's get a visual picture of the relationship between suffering, strength, forgiveness, and joy.

(Break off into groups and act out the following verses)

Psalm 30:11

> *You have turned my mourning into joyful dancing. You have taken away my clothes of mourning and clothed me with joy.*

Romans 15:13

> *I pray that God, who gives you hope, will keep you happy and full of peace as you believe in Him. May you overflow with hope through the power of the Holy Spirit.*

Psalm 32:1–2

> *Oh, what joy for those whose rebellion is forgiven, whose sin is put out of sight! Yes, what joy for those whose record the Lord has cleared of sin, whose lives are lived in complete honesty!*

James 1:2–4 (The Book version)

> *Dear brothers and sisters, whenever trouble comes your way, let it be an opportunity for joy. For when your faith is tested, your endurance has a chance to grow. So let it grow, for when your endurance is fully developed, you will be strong in character and ready for anything.*

As the freshener rejuvenates and revitalizes your skin, confession and repentance will energize and renew joy to your spirit.

Romans 6: 20–23

> *In those days, when you were slaves of sin, you weren't concerned with doing what was right. And what was the result? It was not good, since now you were ashamed of the things you used to do, things that end in eternal doom. But now you are free from the power of sin, and have become slaves of God. Now you do those things that lead to holiness and result in eternal life. For the wages of sin is death, but the free gift of God is eternal life through Jesus Christ, our Lord.*

What was the result of being a slave to sin?

How can sin affect your attitude towards yourself?

What kind of things should you be doing now?

What is the price of sin?

What is God offering instead?

Acts 3:19 (NIV) tells us that when we repent and turn to God, our sins are wiped out and times of refreshing will come from the Lord.

What does Acts 3:19 tell you will happen if you repent and turn to God?

Dictionary.com defines refreshing as

"_____ _____ _____ , or as if with

_____ , _____ , or _____ ;

_____ _____ _____ or

_____ _____ ."

What are some things you think of when you hear the word refresh or refreshing?

How does it make you feel to know that God wants to refresh your spirit?

How did confessing your sins earlier make you feel?

When we walk around feeling the heaviness of disobedience, it will rob us of our energy along with our peace and joy. This will cripple our spiritual walk. If we will drop our heavy sacks of sin at the feet of Jesus, we will find that our strength has been renewed and our vigor for life has been restored.

Take some time to close the session out in prayer and then read some inspirational poetry.

This is an original poem that paints a vivid picture of how sometimes life seems so great and we are on top of the world, then other times it can be a real struggle.

The nature trail of life

In the great cow pasture of life
Sometimes you're the cow
And others you're the patty
Some days you're Miss Bessie
And other days you're just messy
You may get stepped on by Farmer Brown
Then there are times you can paint the town
Sometimes you feel like a cute little bunny
And then there are times when you come out wet and runny
So whether you're the glistening dew
Or you travel around on the bottom of a shoe
Don't be discouraged and don't get blue
Just remember that God always shines on you.

Author- undisclosed

_____

_____

_____

_____

_____

_____

_____

_____

_____

_____

_____

_____

_____

_____

_____

_____

_____

MOISTURIZER

 Saltine Cracker Relay Game

Our faces have now been cleaned down to our pores. The clogged masks have been removed, and our skin has been refreshed. We are now ready for our final step in beauty preparations for this study. We are going to apply the moisturizer and it will hydrate our skin cells and nourish our complexion. It will help guard against environmental causes of dryness and damage.

 Moisturizing Demo

Who has ever had a sunburn? Were you wearing sunscreen? How long were you out in the sun without protection? What did it feel like? Did you sleep well? What happened to your skin a few days later? If we go outside without any sunscreen on, it does not take long before our bodies get burned.

On the great beach of life, if we go out without smearing ourselves with the power and protection of the Holy Spirit, then it won't take long before we're fried like chicken. We need to get in the habit of applying the protective lotion of God's word to our lives. Remember, the spiritual disciplines we discussed earlier? Name some of them.

(Prayer, staying active in church or Christian ministry, faithful friends, mentors...)

Now, those of you who remembered to wear the sunscreen, did any of you end up with a sunburn? How long were you out in the sun? What did it feel like? Did you sleep well? What happened to your skin a few days later? Even when you do remember to put on sunblock if you're outside too long with it, you will still get burned. It still hurts, sleep is no less difficult, and your skin still dries out and peels off.

We may have developed good habits like Bible study and prayer, but if these are simply motions you're going through, then they're just something you're putting on and they're not getting inside, transforming you into who you were destined to be. If we go out and live like the world standards for too long, we will feel the same kinds of pain and can have our lives peeled apart. (Remember the mask we discussed earlier?)

Let's take another look into the lives of the Israelites. After the Lord has set them free from Egyptian slavery in Pharaoh, one would think they would be eternally grateful and anxious to follow the Lord the rest of their days.

Psalm 106: 10–15 (The Message)

He saved them from their life of oppression and prod them loose from the grip of the enemy. Then the waters flowed back on their oppressors; there was not a single survivor. Then they believed His words were true, and broke out in songs of praise, but it wasn't long before they forgot the whole thing. They would not wait to be told what to do. They only cared about pleasing themselves in the desert; they provoked God with their insistent demands. He gave them exactly what they asked for– but along with it, they got an empty heart.

What happens when you decide to do things on your own?

Think of a time when you have strayed from the Lord and found yourself in a difficult situation.

Who did you turn to for help?

Did you try to bargain with God?

If so, what kind of promises did you make?

Which ones have you kept?

How was the situation resolved?

What happens when we only dial God with 911 emergency situations? How would you feel if your friends only called when they needed something, but the rest of the time stepped on you so they could climb higher on the popularity ladder? How will that relationship grow? How often do we do this to those who are in this very room?

What happened to the Babylonians when they sought after their own desires?

Jeremiah 50:38 (The Book)

> *It (judgment) will even strike her water supply,*
> *causing it to dry up. And why? Because the whole*
> *land is filled with idols, and the people are madly in*
> *love with them.*

What are these verses saying?

What will happen to you spiritually when you fill your life with idols?

Look back at the end of Psalm 106:15. Just as the Israelites felt an emptiness in their hearts, there may be times in our life when we have or will experience the same kind of void and we begin looking for things to fill it. This is a symptom of spiritual dehydration.

Have you ever been physically thirsty?

So thirsty you felt like you could spit dust?

What were you craving?

Did you want a thick chocolate shake, soda, milk, an iced latte? Or were you wanting some clean, cold, pure water?

Have you ever had a craving for the living water? Are you like David in Psalm 42:1, which says he longs for God like the deer pants for water?

Just like your physical body craves water when you're thirsty, your spiritual body craves water, whether you recognize it or not.

Sponge Demonstration

I'm sure some of you are feeling about as dry as a desert right now. Our spiritual lives may be like this dry sponge, stiff, brittle, and not being used to reach its potential.

Your life could be like a damp sponge, which has been filled with water at one time, but if it doesn't stay submerged in the water, it will eventually dry out and become brittle again.

A wet sponge shows how important it is to stay saturated and connected to the source of this life-giving water.

What are some practical, everyday ways that you can stay connected?

Will just going to church really do it? What do your friends do to help you in your walk?

When you are not drinking a sufficient amount of H2O every day, then your body tends to not feel as thirsty. But when you get in the habit of drinking plenty of water on a regular basis, then you seem to crave more and more of it. A relationship with the Lord is similar. When we don't have a vital living relationship with the Lord, we really don't understand what we are missing out on. As we give more of ourselves to Him and get to know Him better, we become more eager to deepen our connection with Him. We are not satisfied with just going through the motions of Christianity.

Isaiah 58:11

The Lord will guide you always;
He will satisfy your needs in a sun-scorched land
and will strengthen your frame. You will be like a
well-watered garden,
like a spring whose waters never fail.

List some characteristics of a well watered life.

List the names of people you know who demonstrate these qualities.

Many of us adults are at a point in our lives where we really want to live every minute for the Lord. We so wished we would have done this at a younger age. We would have saved ourselves so many mistakes and heartaches had we realized these things in middle or high school. This would have helped us to stay more grounded in our faith during our college and young adult years. We hope the things we have discussed during this study will really soak into you like a good moisturizer and truly hydrate you so you won't have to experience as many of the life sunburns as we have suffered through.

WRAP UP

When you hear the word beautiful, who do you think of?

What makes a person beautiful?

What is your definition of beauty?

Now look back at the introductory session of your workbook and review your answers you wrote down the first day. Are they the same or has your definition of beauty changed over the course of the study?

When we began our study, we asked the question, what is beauty and where can we find it? Did Ponce de Leon find the fountain that would restore youth? Others today are investing in scientific experiments to preserve their bodies until technology can revive them and restore their youth forever.

Webster's Dictionary defines beauty as "having attractive features and qualities that please."

BUT

True beauty is having features that attract others to Christ and qualities that please the heavenly Father.

The only place we can find lasting beauty is with the one who created it. What is beauty?

> *Psalm 100:5 (The Message)*
>
> **For God is sheer beauty, all– generous in love, loyal always and ever.**

> *Psalm 50:2 (The Message paraphrase)*
>
> **God, the perfection of beauty, shines in glorious radiance.**

These verses tell us that beauty is_____.

Where can we find this beauty?

> *1 Peter 3:4*
>
> **You should be known for the beauty that comes from within, the unfading beauty, of a gentle and quiet spirit, which is so precious to God.**

> *Psalm 89:17a*
>
> **Your vibrant beauty has gotten inside us.**

God's beauty lives inside you in the form of the Holy Spirit. It is through Him and the fruits of the spirit that will transform your heart, mind, and body into the beautiful princess that He knows you are.

He created you to be beautiful and to shine with His glory and splendor. Our spirits should be like diamonds shining with dazzling brilliance. If we've allowed Him to, then the Lord has cleaned us, scraped all the gunk off, and now we're sparkling. If we don't take care, then we will lack shine, and we won't radiate his glory.

Psalm 34:5 says being with Jesus makes you radiant.

Psalm 85:12 says God gives goodness in beauty.

Exodus 34:29–32 says those who have been with Him will shine.

Moses spent 40 days with the Lord on Mount Sinai, when he came off the mountain; his face was radiant with splendor from just being in the presence of God.

The more time spent in an intimate relationship with the Lord, the brighter our lights will shine. When we spend time with Him and get to know Him, then we are like that beacon shining in the night. We will draw others to Him because of our steady, solid relationship we have with Him. Maybe even think of it as an exit sign that points the way out of a dark movie theater, so should we be lighted arrows that point the way out of the darkness of the world, and into the loving light of the Father.

Esther took a year to prepare to meet her king. Through this study we have applied some intense beauty treatments to help prepare us to meet our King. We want to look our best for Him. We want our beauty to shine from the inside out; when we do, He will see us as this verse says:

Psalm 45:11

For your royal husband delights in your beauty; honor him, for he is your Lord.

Proverbs 16:15

When the king smiles there is life, his favor refreshes you like a gentle rain.

**See activitity notes in Appendix for this section

APPENDIX

ANSWER KEY

BEAUTY BASICS

*Webster defines beauty as having **attractive features** and **qualities that please**.*

Cleansing Chapter One

2 Corinthians 6:18–7:1 NLT

> *And I will be your **father** and you will be my **sons** and **daughters**, says the Lord Almighty. Because we have these **promises**, dear friends, let us **cleanse** ourselves from everything that can **defile** our body or spirit. And let us work toward **complete holiness** because we fear God.*

In the above verse, the Strongs word for fear is the Greek word <5401> phobos (fob-os) means

> *"a **wholesome dread of displeasing Him.***

> **The Greek word for "pure" <1571> ekkathairo (ek-kath-ak-ee-ro) means "to clean out, cleanse thoroughly, to purge."**

Have a leader show the clean cloths, and explain that when we confess our sins that Jesus washes them clean and sees them no more.

DEEP CLEANSING

Zondervan Bible dictionary, defines repentance as:

"Being sorry enough about your sins to stop."

Acts 3:19

> *Now turn from your sins and turn to God, so you can be cleansed of your sins.*

Strong's word for "<u>turn</u>" is the Greek word mitanoeo (met-an-o-eh-o) <3340> it is the same word for <u>repent</u> which means:

To change one's **mind** or **purpose**. A **change** for the **better**.

There are three steps involved:

1) gaining new **knowledge**.
2) Regret for your **actions** and a displeasure with **yourself**.
3) A change of **action**.

Strong's word for cleansed is the Greek word exaleipho <1813> (ex-Al-I-fo) this word means:

To **wipe** and **signifies** to **wash** or **smear completely**, to **wipe away**, **wipe off**, completely **remove**.

Psalm 51:17

> *The **sacrifice** you want is a broken **spirit**. A **broken** and **repentant heart** oh, God, you **will not despise**.*

FRESHENER

(Part Two)

Isaiah 40: 29–31

He gives *strength* to the *weary* and increases the *power* of the *weak*. Even *youths* grow *tired* and *weary* and young men *stumble* and *fall*. But those who *hope* in the Lord will *renew* their *strength*. They will *soar* on wings like *eagles* they will run and not grow *weary* they will walk and not be *faint*.

Dictionary.com defines refreshing as "to revive with, or as if, with rest, food, or drink; give new vigor or spirit to."

WRAP UP

These verses tell us that beauty is **God.**

SUPPLY LIST

General:

Books one for each person, including leaders
Ink pens or pencils (can order princess pins from the Internet)
PowerPoint or dry erase board and markers
Music

Facial products:

Facial cleansing product (cream or pre-moistened cloth)
Mask (peel off type works best.)
Freshener/toner
Moisturizer
Washcloths

Beauty Basics

Finger paints
Fingerprint paper
Disposable tablecloths
Paper plates for paint pallets (or you can get small paint pallets at the dollar tree)

Cleansing

White cotton cloths (cut up sheet or discount rack at Walmart.)
Cleanser
Washable markers
Small amount of laundry detergent
Large bowl
Two cups one pretty and dainty that you will make dirty on the inside the other cup broken chipped or dirty on the outside but clean on the inside

Deep Cleansing

Elastic headbands

Plastic or paper mask

Peel off face mask

Sharpie markers

Mask decorating supplies:

Hot glue guns, and glue sticks

Feathers

Sequins

Plastic jewels

Glitter or glitter paint

Picture or cut out of idol (such as the Oscar award use two per girl)

Fire pit or small disposable barbecue grill

__optional idea__ *New, shiny penny glued to a piece of paper with the phrase "what are you hanging onto?"*

Fire starter log and/or wood Lighter or matches

Freshener (parts one and two)

Small hand mirrors. (can order cute princess mirrors online.

Fake money (realistic as possible)

$20 bill (S)

Freshener or skin toner

Two backpacks (one stuffed with paper, the other with heavy books)

Ankle weights— one set

Armor of God clings or cards

Moisturizer

Water bottles with John 7:37b "if anyone is thirsty, let him come to me and drink"– Jesus

Bottle of Moisturizer

Saltine crackers for relay game

Other salty snacks to increase thirstiness

Table top water fountain on display (if possible)

3 sponges

Wrap Up
Fragrance candles
A rose for each girl (if possible)
Chonda Pierce "four eyed blind" CD, TRACK 8–9

Suggested songs:
"Come to the Altar" or "Give Us Clean Hands" – (Cleansing)
"Let It Rise" – (Deep Cleansing)
"Hunger and Thirst" by Henry Seeley – (Moisturizer)
"Come to the River" – (Moisturizer)
"There is a Fountain" – (Moisturizer)
"You Say" by Laura Daigle or "Mercy Saw Me" by Chonda Pierce – (Wrap Up)

> **Leaders please be creative here and choose songs that will speak to your individual group**

GAMES AND ACTIVITIES

These will be clearly marked in each section where you are encouraged to use these suggestions or something similar to get the point across.

BEAUTY BASICS - SECTION 1

Fingerpainting: *Give each girl a sheet of finger-paint paper and instruct them to paint a picture of something beautiful. It could be a flower, the ocean, whatever comes to mind when they think of the word beauty. Give them 10 minutes or so to complete the project. These can be used for their placemats if a meal is provided.*

Purpose: *To get them thinking about what beauty is and also as an object lesson about sinful behavior that will be discussed more thoroughly in Section One, Cleansing.*

Optional Summer Activity: Mud Volleyball

Purpose: *This is an object lesson about sinful behavior that will be discussed more thoroughly in Section One, Cleansing.*

CLEANSING – SECTION 2

Cleansing Demonstration: *Select one girl from your group to be your cleansing model. Have your "spa technician" cleanse the model's face, while another leader reads the first paragraph of the section. After the model's face is clean, hand out cleanser to each girl and have them clean their faces. (Encourage all girls to participate in all these activities)*

Purpose: *To get each girl involved in the study and also to use as a reference point during the lesson on cleansing.*

Dirty Cup Demo: *Bring out a tray with two cups on it, one cup will be fancy fine china clean and beautiful on the outside but very dirty and grimy on the inside, the other cup will be a plain coffee mug, unattractive possibly broken or chipped with dirt and paint all over the outside, but perfectly clean on the inside. Make sure the audience doesn't see the inside of the cups, offer a cup of water to one of the girls and ask her which cup she wants you to pour her water into. She will most likely pick the pretty and clean cup, but when she sees how dirty it is, she will not want to drink from it.*

Purpose: *To emphasize the point that your inner cleanliness of the heart is more important than how you look on the outside.*

Sins Demo: *Give each girl a piece of white fabric and a washable marker. As they go to have some time alone with their Father God, have them write down any sins that they need to confess to Him. When they return for group time, have a leader standing with a bowl of water that each girl will drop their cloth into. During praise and worship time have the leader put some detergent into a bowl and make sure cloths come clean. After praise and worship time, show the girls their clean cloths.****

Purpose: *To give the girls a visual understanding of how God takes our confessed sins and washes us clean.*

***NOTE-Explain to the girls that just like the cloths were dirty with sin and are now sparkling clean, so are we when confession is made to Jesus. He sees our sins no more.

DEEP CLEANSING – SECTION 3

Facial Deep Cleansing Demo: *Choose another "model" from the group. Have the "spa technician" apply the facial mask on "model". Hand out headbands and a sufficient amount of mask gel to cover their faces. Have girls leave mask solution on until well set and continue with lesson while girls are wearing the masks.*

(A great photo op time is while students have on their masks)

Masquerade Activity: *Give each girl a plastic or paper mask and a marker. Instruct them to write on the inside of the mask some reasons that make people wear masks. (Examples: to be popular, to fit in, to hide insecurities....) During free time (if doing this as a weekend getaway) girls will decorate their mask with feathers, sequins, beads, paint, etc.....*

If doing this as a weekly study allow time to decorate before finishing lesson or after lesson is done

Purpose: *Hands on learning tool, to get them thinking about their own lives and the mask they possibly are wearing. This will also serve as a reminder to them when they get home or during their weekly activities.*

(Suggested Activity: Have a masquerade ball and let the girls wear their masks)

Idol Activity: *Give each girl two pieces of "idol paper" instruct them to write on the first sheet one or more things that God would consider an idol in their life, on the second sheet write down active ways to guard against idolatry. Have girls take the first sheet (their idols) outside and throw them into a prepared fire. Have girls join hands around the fire and spend some time in prayer silently and then together.*

Purpose: *To help girls recognize idols they have in their own lives and the importance of giving them up.*

FRESHENER (PART 1) SECTION 4

Freshener Demo: *Choose "model" and have the "spa technician" apply freshener to her while a leader reads paragraph two in the Freshener section. Have all other girls apply freshener.*

Before you begin the Affirmation Game have one of your leaders share about how God has used their weaknesses for His Glory.

Affirmation Game: *Divide girls into groups of 5-6 and have one person start and tell the person on the right something positive and affirming and continue around the circle until each girl has been positively affirmed.*

Money Game: *Have leaders hide real and fake $20 bills around the room and whoever finds it gets to keep it. (Don't tell them some of the money is fake) while the girls are searching for the money have the leaders try to distract them in their search by telling them the money isn't real, asking them to go do something else instead of searching for the money, asking them to help with something, get creative to try to distract them on their search.*

You may want to attach scripture verses for added emphasis on the back of the money.

Real Money:	*Jeremiah 29:13*
	Psalm 63:1
	1 Chronicles 16:11
Fake Money:	*Proverbs 22:1*
	Proverbs 11:28
	Ecclesiastes 5:10

You don't have to use all these verses. If there are other verses that would speak better to your group, use those.

Purpose: *To emphasize the point that we need to seek the Lord with more passion than we seek popularity, money, or boyfriends.*

FRESHENER – (PART 2) SECTION 5

Race with Weights: *Choose six girls three for team A and three for team B. (You may want to choose the three fastest girls for team A and non-athletic girls for team B). Have a coach for each team to get them suited up for the relay race. Team A will have a backpack stuffed with paper. Team B will have a backpack filled with books or other heavy objects and will have ankle weights. Set up the race as an obstacle course or up and down stairs or along a straight away. After the first runner on each team is done with her race, have her pass her backpack to the next runner. Do this for each of the team members until all girls have run the race.*

Purpose: *To show how burdens in life can weigh us down if we choose to carry them alone.*

MOISTURIZER SECTION 6

How Thirsty Are You: *If you have a "free time" before beginning this section, to add emphasis you can take away all liquid refreshments for about 2 hours or so and give them plenty of salty snacks to munch on. You will need to put all the cups/water bottles away and hide the drinks, the girls will get desperate for water. The leaders will all have glasses of ice water in the beginning of this section.*

Saltine Cracker Relay: *Divide the girls into teams and give each girl a saltine cracker, the first person in line has to chew up and swallow the cracker, then whistle to signal the next girl to start her cracker and so on.*

Purpose: *To make girls experience physical thirst to enhance the lesson on spiritual thirst and dryness.*

Moisturizer Demo: *Select a new "model" from the group and have the "spa tech" apply moisturizer while the leader reads the first paragraph of the Moisturizer section. Then give each girl moisturizer to apply to their faces.*

Sponge Demo: *Have three sponges on hand, one dry and brittle, one moistened but not wet, and another in a bowl of water. Each of them will be explained during the designated point in the lesson. Show each sponge as you are explaining it.*

WRAP UP – SECTION 6

Play the 8th and 9th track from Chonda Pierce's Four Eyed Blonde album or another option would be to play track 8 of Chonda Pierce then play "You Say" by Lauren Daigle. You can play it from YouTube or access it from www.skindeepbiblestudy.com.

After the story when she begins singing have leaders hand out roses to each of the girls telling them something affirming about them personally and how loved they are.

End with prayer thanking God for each girl's beauty and uniqueness.

MOVIE SCRIPT AND SKITS

Desire and deception
A three-part saga

Characters   **Costumes**

David- Crown, big glasses, fake teeth, cape, maybe overalls
Bathie- Long wig, dress and towel. For extra humor, have a super buff guy that the girls all know to play this part.
Guard- Hat, cape, stick
Uriah- Wearing camo
Nathan- cheap goodwill suit with the tv preacher hair

Feel free to change the name of towns here to places your girls would be more familiar with.

Our actors were men in leadership (youth minister, worship leader…) the girls knew and were familiar with. Would also be fun to have guys from the youth group acting this out as well.
When working on this think Beverly Hillbillies

Our version of this video is on our website and we encourage you to watch it for ideas to create your own.

Desire and Deception
Part One
(2 Sam 11:2-4)

David: oh, doggies lookie there at that hot babe

Guard: (*looks through toy binoculars*) you betcha, she's purtier than a pig snout (*camera scans to Bathie in shower*)

Bathie: (*singing in the shower*) oh, what a beautiful morning...

David: guard, who is that there pretty little filly?

Guard: that's Uriah's old lady. You know the one from Grundy county? (**pick a town or place your girls are familiar with that everyone jokes they wouldn't want to be from**)

David: yeah, he's off feudin with them Soddy boys (**insert another rowdy place here**), go fetch her for me!

Guard: yes, king as you wish. (*guard goes to get Bathie*)

Guard: (to Bathie) the king wants to see you

Bathie: give me a minute, Mr. guard; I need to make sure I look my best for the king (*looking in the mirror fixing up for king, but you can only see her from the back you haven't seen her face at this point*)

Guard brings Bathie to Palace, David and Bathie run in slow motion to one another and embrace,

After embrace

David: come up to my hayloft my pretty little pony

End Part One

Desire and Deception
Part Two
(2 Samuel 11:5–27)

Bathie calls David on the phone to tell him she's pregnant

Bathie: Davey, baby, we're gonna have us a young'un

David: *(as he hangs up the phone)* oh no, I'm in more trouble than a turkey on thanksgivin'. Guard, bring me Uriah from the feudin' grounds.

Uriah enters

David: sounds like that feudin's been rough, I can see you need to go home to that pretty little phillie of yours, I'm sure she's been missing you something awful

We see Uriah laying down in front of the palace doors.

The next day...

David: why did you sleep on the ground when you had a nice warm bed waiting for you last night?

Uriah: I couldn't possibly enjoy a night at home with my boyz sleeping in army tents

David: come on in here and have you some fried possum and granny's special recipe

Uriah and David sit down at a table to eat Uriah turns up a bottle with XXX on it

Uriah: this stuff burns when it goes down (*Uriah is stumbling out*),

David: you go on home now, ya hear?

Uriah is seen sleeping in front of the doors again

David seals a letter

David: that should take care of Uriah

Uriah: (*skipping off to war*) I bet this letter has orders for my promotion!!! (*he says excitedly*)

Show hands opening letter close-up on the words

> *Joab,*
>
> *Put Uriah in the front line, where the fighting is the fiercest, then withdraw from him so he will be struck down and die.*
>
> *King David*

Guard: King David I have some bad news to report, the feudin got rough last night. Uriah got killed.

David: Well, that happens when in feuding times, I guess the honorable thing to do is bring his widow here to live and I'll take care of her.

End Part Two

Desire and Deception
Part three
(2 Sam 12:1–13)

Scene opens with Nathan and David talking

David: hey Ole buddy, come sit a spell with me.

Nathan: I've got a situation to tell you about

David: Tell it like it is

Nathan: well, there were these two pumpkin farmers one had a field as far as you could see just plum full of big orange pumpkins, the other guy had one scrawny little vine, but he watered that vine and talked to it, like it was somp'in special. That little vine finally gave him the prettiest pumpkin you ever did see, why would why it would've won him a blue ribbon at the county fair *(David is listening with interest in reacting to it)*. One day, the president of John Deere tractors came a callin' on the rich farmer

David: you don't say
Nathan: Yep, sure enough he did. You know what he told the Farmer?
David: What?

Nathan: He wanted some dessert. You know what his favorite dessert was?

David: No, what?

Nathan: Pumpkin pie

David: Naw, really?

Nathan: Yep, pumpkin pie, you know what he did?

David: Tell me

Nathan: The rich man sent his wife to go, steal the poor man's only precious pumpkin, because he was too greedy to use one of his own pumpkins to make a pie.

David: *(visibly upset interrupts the story)* that's the lowest thing I ever did hear of, that rich man ought to be hog, tied and throwed in the creek

Nathan: David, that rich man is you; you had a roll in the hay with Uriah's old lady then you dug his grave

David: *(says remorsefully)* You're right, I've been badder than ole King Kong and meaner than a junkyard dog. *(Bows his head in shame.)* I have and I have sinned against God.

The End

Characters for Adam and Eve skit:
Adam
Eve
Serpent

Adam and Eve
Part One

Room is set up with various fruits, arranged on a table. In the middle of the table, sitting much higher on a pedestal are some bananas, sitting on a tray. If possible, have some type of lighting on them. Adam and Eve are dressed in totally out of date clothing. Serpent/Satan is dressed in snakeskin type clothing looking very cool

Eve: Wow, look at all this fruit. It looks so good and I'm very hungry. What shall I try today? *(Pick up grapes.)* Yum!! These look good.

Serpent: *(interrupting Eve)* Oh Eve, you are looking very lovely today.

Eve: Thank you, Mr. Serpent. Would you like to have a snack with me?

Serpent: Sure, I would be honored– here. Let me find you something, especially delicious. I've sampled them all you know.

Eve: That would be great, you know Adam never even offers to fix dinner for me.

Serpent: Now, here is the tastiest fruit in the garden. *(Reaches for the bananas, peels one and takes a bite makes eyes roll back as if it's the most spectacular thing ever)* Oh, mmmmmmm, this is absolutely heavenly. You've got to try this. You know they say bananas are the world's most perfect fruit.

Eve: *(her mouthwatering)* No, I better not, God told Adam and I that we weren't allowed to eat that one

Serpent: What?? Really?? Did he say that? None of the fruit in the garden? God says you mustn't eat any of it?

Eve: Of course, we can eat it, all of it, except the fruit in the center of the garden

Serpent: Are you sure this is the one he was talking about? (*Running the banana under eves nose*)

Eve: (*licking her lips*) Yes, I'm pretty sure that's the one. He said we could eat all these other fruits, just not that one. He said, if we did, we would die (*very dramatically*).

Serpent: That's a lie. You will not die. (*laughing*) God knows the instant you eat it you will be just like him your eyes will be open, and you will know good from evil. Come on, one little bite won't kill you.

Eve: It does look and smell wonderful.

Serpent: Like I said, it's the best fruit in the garden

Eve: Well, you have already peeled it for me. I would hate to see it go to waste. A couple little bites couldn't hurt anything.

Eve eats the banana and peels another and gives it to Adam. They both look at each other and gasp covering their mouths and say;

Adam and Eve: Oh, look at those horrible clothes, we need to go the mall, we're so out of style!! (*As they run out of the room, the serpent laughs at them.*)

End part one

Characters
Adam
Eve
Serpent
God (voice only)

Adam and Eve
Part Two

Adam and Eve enter, they are covered in blankets or wraps– sheepishly walking around. The character of God is voice only.

God: Adam, Eve, where are you two? It's time for our afternoon stroll in the garden.

When they hear the voice of God, they both run under the table and hide so the audience can see them

God: Adam??? Eve??? Where are you?

Adam: We're over here, Lord…

God: Why are you hiding?

Adam: Because we're so unstylish and embarrassed

God: You are out of style??

Adam: I'm afraid so, Lord.

God: Come out and talk to Me *(Adam and Eve crawl out from under the table.)* Who told you that you were not stylish?

Adam: Well, uhmmmm…

God: Adam, did you disobey Me and eat from the banana tree?

Adam: *(pushes Eve away from him and points at her)* it was all her fault, Lord, she made me do it. Yeah, this woman that you gave me, she made me eat one of those bananas.

God: Eve, what do you have to say for yourself?

Eve: *(giving Adam the evil eye,)* the devil made me do it***Or*** It was the serpent he made me do it, he tricked me. He said it was okay.

All freeze

The End

Characters:
Missionary Megan
Patti Purity
Tiffany Trustworthy
Bossy Briana- part two only
Debbie Downes

Parade of Fakes
Part One

Characters should wear a sign around their neck with their "name "on it

Megan and Patty enter room

Patti: (*To Megan*) So how was your mission trip to Cambodia?

Megan: oh, it was great! Our team worked at an orphanage teaching sign language to kids. In the evenings we would go down to the city dump and share Christ with the homeless people, and then we would stay up all night doing repairs to homes that have been damaged from a bad storm.

Patti: That all sounds so tiring, but I'm sure it was worth it.

Megan: We had great results. I was able to witness to 24 people and my team altogether led 86 people to the Lord.

Patti: Wow, that's awesome! You do so much for others, Megan, what is that your fourth overseas mission trip you've been on?

Megan: (*getting a little prideful*) that was my fifth, but who's counting?

Debbie walks in looking very sad, Patti and Megan just look at her and then try to act like she isn't there.

Debbie: (*sadly*) Hey Megan, hey Patty

Megan and Patti mutter hi to Debbie then look at each other and roll their eyes and continue their own conversation

Megan: So, what's been going on with you while I've been gone? Are you still going out with Kyle?

Patti: Oh, yes, we've been going out for over a month now!

Megan: Just be careful I hear a lot of girls know him, if you know what I mean

Patti: don't worry, if he ever tries anything with me, I'll let him know real quick that I've been to the "True Love Waits" rally three years in a row! Anyway, I'm not like those other girls he's dated.

Megan: looking at her watch, I've got to go, tonight is our monthly missionary club meeting and I'm in charge of refreshments

Patti: Bye, talk to you later Meg

Megan leaves and Patti is left alone with Debbie. Patti and Debbie freeze.

End scene one

Parade of Fakes
Part two

Tiffany enters carrying books and sits down next to Debbie acting sympathetic to her

Tiffany: Hey Deb, what's wrong?

Debbie: My parents got into this big fight last night.

Tiffany: Oh no, what happened?

Debbie: My dad got mad and left, I don't think he's ever coming home again

Tiffany: (*hugs Debbie then tries to reassure her*) I know it seems bad now, but my parents have done that before, maybe your dad just needed to get away and cool off for a while. I bet he'll be back soon.

Debbie: (*Perking up a little*) You really think so?

Tiffany: Sure

Debbie: Well, thanks for listening. Please don't tell anyone about this, okay?

Tiffany: Oh, of course not, I would never break your confidence!

Debbie exits and Briana enters. When Debbie leaves Tiffany puts her books down in Debbie's spot.

Briana: (*In a bossy tone to Tiffany*) Tiff, don't forget the Y-Teens meeting after school today. You need to be there since you skipped last week. You're supposed to be the secretary and take notes- I couldn't plan well for this meeting because I didn't have notes from last time. (*Pushing books out-of-the-way, and helping herself to a seat next to Tiffany*) move your stuff out of the way, I need to sit down, my feet are killing me, I thought these hundred-dollar shoes were supposed to feel good. So, what were you talking to **that** girl about?

Tiffany: Well, she asked me not to tell anyone, but… *(Both girls lean together as Tiffany is going to tell her something. They both freeze)*

Patty: (off to side, on her phone) Hello…, Yes, this is Patty…, Oh hello Dr. Bates…, What!?? You have to be kidding…. I can't have a baby!!! *(She freezes)*

All actors stay frozen for a few seconds, and quietly exit as lesson continues

The End

www.ingramcontent.com/pod-product-compliance
Lightning Source LLC
Chambersburg PA
CBHW051548120626
46551CB00013B/1413